ANYONE CAN READ, WRITE, SPEAK BETTER

A Guide to English Literacy Proficiency

Copyright © 2024 by Godwin Essang.
All rights reserved.

Introduction

This handbook is an excellent guide for teaching adults' English learners how to read, write and spell proficiently. It is Designed specifically for adults with little or no formal education or adults from non-English speaking background who are eager to develop English reading, writing, spelling and speaking skills.

We understand that everyone's path to education is unique, and this book will make that path as clear and enjoyable as possible.

In the pages that follow, you will find a roadmap, a guide, and practical activities all in one. We have broken down this handbook into manageable lessons, each carefully crafted to help the learners build their English literacy skills step by step. No fancy jargons here, just straightforward, practical guidance.

**To the Instructor
How to Use This Book and
Get the Best Out of It:**

1. **Start from the Beginning:** Begin with the sounds table, followed by "Working with sounds" and then the rest of the chapters. Each week builds upon the knowledge gained in the previous one.

2. **Preparation is Key:** Take some time to familiarize yourself with each week's content before teaching it. Review the objectives, examples, and exercises.

3. Engage Your Learners:
Encourage active participation. Ask questions, initiate discussions, and create a supportive and interactive learning environment.

4. Practice, Practice, and Practice:
Repetition is crucial in language learning. Encourage learners to practice what they've learned, both during the sessions and as homework assignments.

5. Patience and Encouragement:
Learning to read, write and speak can be challenging, and progress

may vary among learners. Be patient, offer encouragement, and celebrate small victories.

6. **Keep it Fun:**
Learning should be an enjoyable experience. Incorporate games, stories, and creative activities to make the lessons engaging and memorable.

Table of Content

Introduction - - - 2

Table of Contents - - 3

Chapter 1:
Letters and Sounds
Orientation - - - 9
Introduction to Phonics - 12

Chapter 2:
Working with Sounds - 15
Why Certain Letters Have Multiple
Sounds - - - - 17

Chapter 3:
Grapheme and Phoneme - 52

Chapter 4:
Sound Syllables - - 72
Counting Syllables - - 79

Syllable stress - - 88

Chapter 5:
Levels of Phonemics Awareness
- - - - - 82
Graphemes with Similar Sounds -
- - - - - 87

Chapter 6:
Introduction to Sight words
- - - - - - 90
Sight Words Sentences - 93
Sentence Formation - - 95

Chapter 7:
Punctuation - - - 97

Chapter 8: Reading Comprehension - - 102

Activities - - - - 111

Chapter 1: Letters and Sounds Orientation

For proper understanding, note the following;

1. The alphabet has 26 letters. They are made of uppercase (capital letters) and the lowercase (small letters) e.g., Aa, Bb, Cc.

2. Each of the letters represents a sound which is also called phoneme.

3. Though, there are 26 alphabet letters, but these letters produced 44 sounds. The reason is because;
a. Some of the letters have more than one sound. The change in

a letter sound happens mostly because of another letter that is before or after it.

b. Secondly, two or more letters may come together to produce one particular sound.

4. The name of a letter is different from its sound.

For example;

By name, these letters are called a, b, c, d.

But by sound, they are /a/, /b/, /c/, /d/

In summary, the letter's name is what we call the letter while the letter's sound is the sound the letter makes when it is used in a word.

From the above explanation, we can see that words are made up of sounds, and sounds are made by letters. For example, 'bad' which has /b/, /a/, /d/ sounds combination.

Therefore, in learning to read, the main focus should be on the letter sounds.

Although there are 44 sounds, but in this book, we have over 60 sounds. This is because we simplify the sounds for a quicker understanding.

Introduction to Phonics

Phonics is a method of teaching reading to learners by linking sounds and the letters or symbols that represent those sounds. It focuses on the relationship between individual sound (phoneme) and the letters (graphemes) or syllables.

From the above definition, we have identified three elements of phonics; graphemes, phonemes and syllables. These three tools work together and we are going to utilize them in subsequent topics. But first let's consider their meaning and functions.

Elements of phonics

The three elements of phonics:

1. Grapheme

A grapheme is a visual symbol or letter that represents a specific sound or group of sounds in a language. For example, in the English language, the letter "a" is a grapheme that represents the sound /æ/ in words like cat, bat, or the sound /ei/ in words like "cake". This is to say that all the letters of the alphabet are graphemes because they represent sounds.

2. Phoneme

A phoneme is a smallest unit of sound in a spoken language that distinguishes one word from another. For example, the word "man" has three phonemes /m/, /a/, /n/ and "baby" has four phonemes /b/, /ei/, /b/, /i/.

Phonemes come together to form words and there 44 phonemes (sounds) in the English language which are represented by symbols known as graphemes. For the purpose of avoiding some of the abstract symbols used in the 44 sounds, only the symbols (letters) use in reading and writing will be used in this book.

Chapter 2: Working with Sounds

Proper knowledge of the letter sounds is the foundation for developing reading skills, most especially for adult English learners. The reason why this is important to adult learners is because adults easily establish clarity and flow in learning when there is consistency in the attributes or characteristics of the elements learning about

For example, if an adult learner learns that /a/ is the sound of letter "a", they will definitely want to associate the sound /a/ to letter "a" in all context. But we know that in English that the letter "a" have different sounds based on the context it is applied.

Therefore, it is important to thoroughly treat letter sounds and their context-based dynamic nature.

Why Certain Letters Have Multiple Sounds

In this chapter, we are going to consider the letters with more than one sound and the context to which the changes in sounds of these letters occur.

Here are a few general reasons why certain letters may change their sounds.

• The place occupied by a letter (sound) in a particular word may influence the sound it produces. For example, the sound of "e" is often silent when it is at the end of a word with more than two syllables. The primary function of "e" being the last letter of a word is to change the sound of the preceding vowel from a short to a long sound.

For example:
   a. Hat -   hate
   b. Cut -   cute
   c. Can -   cane

• The presence and position of a particular sound or letter may change the sound of another. From the previous examples we can see that the presence of "e" and it position changes the sound of other vowels from short to long sounds. Let take a look at more examples.

For example:

a. Sow -   show
b. Bid -   bird
c. Rack -   race

From the above examples, you can see that the presence of "h" and being next to "s" changes the sound of "s" to "sh".

Also, the presence and position of "r" changes the sound of "i".

Now let's explore each of these letters with multiple sounds and the context to which the changes happen.

1. Letter "c"

The letter "c" may sound as "s" such as in "cease, rice, Cyril" and can also function as "k" such as in "cat, car, cut".

If you observe very well, you will notice that "c" produces the "s" sound when it is followed by "i", "y" and "e" ("ci, cy, and ce").

More examples:

a. ce - cent, ceiling, celebrity, cell

b. ci - city, cinema, circle, precise

c. cy -cycle, cylinder, fancy, mercy.

In other cases, such as when "c" is followed by "a", "o", "u" or any of the consonant letters, it usually produces a "/k/" sound.
For example: cut, cat, cot, cry, club.
However, there are a few exceptions to point out. There are cases where "c" followed by certain consonants or specific combinations results in different sounds.

For example:

a. "cious" pronounced as "shus". This is found in words like, delicious, gracious, vicious, precious etc.

b. "ch" pronounced as "tsh". This is found in words like, chair, cheese, chocolate, choice etc.
c. "cion" and "cian" pronounced as "shin". These are found in words like, suspicion, clinician, musician.

These are common variations found in "c". each of the context should be properly taught to help them avoid mix up and mispronunciation.

2. Letter "i"

The letter "i" is one of the letters with various sounds based on certain defined context.

Let's break it down;

a. The short /i/ (short "i")
this is found in words with short closed syllabled. For example, when "i" appears in short words or syllable closed by a consonant, it usually produces the short /i/ sound.

For example; bit, sit, fix, mix, rich.

Also, "i" can make the /i/ sound unstressed syllables, particularly in longer words.

For example; animal, family, limit etc.

b. /ai/ sound (long "i")

The /ai/ sound occurs in the following situations;

- Open syllables: when "i" is followed by a vowel or at the end of a syllable, it often produces the /ai/ sound.

For example; idle, idea, item etc.

- Silent "e" rule: in words where "i" is followed by a consonant and then silent "e", it often makes the /ai/ sound.

For example; bike, time, fine, size

- Before certain consonant combinations:

In some words, "i" before certain consonant clusters (like "nd" or "ld") can also produce the /ai/ sound.

Example; find, kind, wild, child etc.

c. r- controlled "i"
this is a situation in which "r" significantly influences the pronunciation of "i" especially when "r" is preceded by "i". in this case "ir" produces /3:r/ (like "eh") sound.

Example; bird, first, girl, shirt, sir etc.

Note the following exceptions:
- if "ir" is a part of a multisyllabic word or followed by certain consonant, the "i" often retains the short /i/ sound before the "r".

Examples; mirror, spirit, miracle, irritate etc.

- in some words, particularly in American English, "ir" can be part of a diphthong, producing /air/ sound.

Examples; fire, tire, hire etc.

The pronunciation of "ir" can change significantly depending on the word and regional accent. But the above context are the most common patterns that English language learners are like to encounter.

3. Letter "y"

The letter "y" in English can produce three common vowel sounds which include,
- /ai/ (long "i" sound) as in fly, dry
- /i/ (long "e" sound) as in baby, lazy

"y" typically produces the /i/ in the following context;

i. In the middle of a word: when "y" appears in the middle of words, it often takes the /i/ sound especially in shorter, unstressed syllables. Eg. gym, myth, system symbol, lyrics etc.

ii. "y" in prefixes and suffixes: in some words where "y" appears in prefixes and suffixes, it can produce the /i/ sound. Eg. typical, analyst, dynasty.

iii. "y" as /a/ sound (long "i"): the /ai/ sound usually occurs when "y" is;

- "y" at the end of a word, particularly in monosyllabic words (one syllable words) or open syllable, it often makes the /ai/ sound. Eg. fly, cry, try, sky, etc.

- "y" can also make the /ai/ sound in multisyllabic words when it forms part of the syllable that has emphasis. Eg. comply, multiply, apply etc.
- If the syllable containing "y" is stressed, it is more likely to produce the /ai/ sound.
- In multisyllabic words where "y" appears at the end, it often produces the /i/ sound, especially when the preceded vowel is an open syllable (ending in vowel). Eg. baby, happy, candy, city etc.

4. The Letter "a"

The letter "A" can produce several sounds depending on its position, surrounding letters, and syllable stress.

a. */æ/ Sound (as in "cat"):* Typically occurs in short, stressed syllables where "a" is followed by a consonant. The short /æ/ sound is common in closed syllables (syllables that end in a consonant).
Examples: cat, bat, hat.

b. */eɪ/ Sound (as in "cake")*

- **Context:** Occurs in open syllables or when "a" is followed by a silent "e," creating a long vowel sound.

Examples: cake, lake, make

The silent "e" at the end of these words modifies the vowel sound, making it long.

/ɑː/ *Sound (as in "father")*

- **Context:** Often occurs in words where "a" is followed by "r" or in certain open syllables.

Examples: father, calm, car.

The "r" following "a" (known as r-colored vowel influence) lengthens the sound, giving it an "ah" quality.

/ə/ Sound (as in "sofa")

- **Context:** Occurs in unstressed syllables, where the "a" takes on a schwa sound, which is the most neutral vowel sound.

- **Examples:** sofa, banana, about

In unstressed syllables, vowels often reduce to a schwa sound, making them quicker and less distinct.

/ɔː/ Sound (as in "water")

- **Context:** Found in some dialects, especially in British English, when "a" precedes "l" or "r."

- **Examples:** water, talk, salt

The influence of "l" or "r" in certain accents causes a broader, rounder sound.

5. The Letter "E"

The letter "E" has several variations in sound depending on its position and the letters around it.

/e/ Sound (as in "bed")

- **Context:** Found in short, stressed syllables where "e" is followed by a consonant.

- **Examples:** bed, red, set.

The short /e/ sound occurs in closed syllables where vowels are generally short.

/iː/ *Sound (as in "be")*

- **Context:** Occurs in open syllables or when "e" is at the end of a word.

Examples: be, she, he.

In open syllables, where the vowel is at the end of the syllable, the sound is often long.

/ə/ *Sound (as in "taken")*

- **Context:** Happens in unstressed syllables, leading to a schwa sound.

Examples: taken, problem, happen

The schwa sound is common in unstressed syllables, making the vowel sound more neutral.

Silent "E" (as in "bake")

- **Context:** When "e" is at the end of a word but is silent, it typically makes the preceding vowel long.

- **Examples:** bake, hide, hope

The silent "e" rule changes the preceding vowel sound to its long form.

6. The Letter "O"

The letter "O" can make various sounds depending on the context.

/ɒ/ Sound (as in "pot")

- **Context:** Common in British English when "o" appears in short, stressed syllables.
- **Examples:** pot, hot, not
- In closed syllables, the short /ɒ/ sound is typical, especially in British accents.

/oʊ/ Sound (as in "go")

- **Context:** Found in open syllables or when "o" is followed by a consonant and silent "e."

- **Examples:** go, no, hope

The open syllable or silent "e" makes the "o" sound long.

/uː/ Sound (as in "do")

- **Context:** Occurs in some short words, especially function words.
- **Examples:** do, who, lose.

Irregular vowel pronunciation due to historical changes in English pronunciation.

/ʌ/ Sound (as in "love")

- **Context:** When "o" appears in stressed syllables and is followed by certain consonants.
- **Examples:** love, come, money

This sound often occurs due to vowel reduction in stressed syllables, making it closer to a /ʌ/ sound.

/ɔː/ Sound (as in "or")

- **Context:** When "o" is followed by "r," creating an r-colored vowel sound.

- **Examples:** or, horse, more

The presence of "r" alters the vowel sound, giving it a rounded quality.

7. The Letter "U"

"U" can have several distinct sounds, often depending on its position and the letters around it.

/ʌ/ Sound (as in "cup")

- **Context:** Appears in stressed syllables when followed by a consonant.
- **Examples:** cup, luck, fun

The short /ʌ/ sound occurs in closed syllables where vowels are generally short.

/uː/ Sound (as in "flute")

- **Context:** When "u" is in an open syllable or followed by a silent "e."

- **Examples:** flute, June, rule

The open syllable or silent "e" extends the vowel to its long form.

/juː/ Sound (as in "cute")
- **Context:** When "u" follows "c," "d," "t," or other consonants, especially at the beginning of a word or syllable.
- **Examples:** cute, use, music

The consonant influences the vowel sound, resulting in a glide to /juː/.

/ʊ/ Sound (as in "put")
- **Context:** Occurs in closed syllables with specific consonants.
- **Examples:** put, push, pull

The /ʊ/ sound is common in closed syllables but is less frequent than /ʌ/ for "u."

8. The Letter "G"

The letter "G" can produce different sounds depending on what follows it.

/g/ Sound (as in "go")

- **Context:** When "g" is followed by "a," "o," "u," or a consonant.

- **Examples:** go, game, gum.

This is the hard "g" sound, typical when followed by vowels "a," "o," "u," or any consonant.

/dʒ/ Sound (as in "giant")

- **Context:** When "g" is followed by "e," "i," or "y."
- **Examples:** giant, gem, gym.

The soft "g" sound occurs before "e," "i," or "y," similar to how "c" changes before these letters.

Silent "G" (as in "gnome")

- **Context:** When "g" is followed by "n" at the start of a word or syllable.
- **Examples:** gnome, gnaw, sign

The "g" becomes silent due to historical spelling conventions where "gn" words were once pronounced with a hard "g".

9. The Letter "S"

The letter "S" can produce multiple sounds, depending on its context within a word.

/s/ Sound (as in "sit")

- **Context:** Found in most positions, especially at the start of words or when followed by a consonant.
- **Examples:** sit, snake, sun

The standard /s/ sound occurs most frequently when "s" starts a word or appears before a consonant.

/z/ Sound (as in "has")

- **Context:** When "s" follows a vowel or is between vowels.
- **Examples:** has, is, busy

The /z/ sound happens often due to the influence of surrounding vowels, which can voice the "s".

/ʃ/ Sound (as in "sugar")

- **Context:** When "s" is followed by "h" or occurs in certain word forms.
- **Examples:** sugar, sure, pressure

In certain contexts, often influenced by French origins, "s" shifts to /ʃ/.

/ʒ/ Sound (as in "measure")

- **Context:** Found in words of French origin, particularly in the middle or end of words.
- **Examples:** measure, vision, leisure.

The /ʒ/ sound often appears in loanwords where the pronunciation shifts to match the original language's phonetics.

10. The Letter "X"

The letter "X" can represent different sounds depending on its position.

/ks/ Sound (as in "box")

- **Context:** Occurs most frequently in the middle or at the end of words.

- **Examples:** box, mix, fix

This combination of /k/ and /s/ is the most common pronunciation of "x."

/gz/ Sound (as in "exam")

- **Context:** When "x" appears at the beginning of words or between vowels.

- **Examples:** exam, example, exact.

The /gz/ sound occurs because of the voicing influence of the vowels around "x."

/z/ Sound (as in "xylophone")

- **Context:** Found mainly in Greek-origin words or scientific terms.
- **Examples:** xylophone, xenon

The pronunciation shifts to /z/ due to Greek roots, where "x" often represented a /z/ sound.

11. The Letter "T"

The letter "T" changes its sound based on surrounding letters and its position.

/t/ Sound (as in "top")

- **Context:** Found in most standard uses, especially at the start of words or when followed by a consonant.

- **Examples:** top, bat, table.

The basic /t/ sound is most common in English, representing a voiceless stop.

/ʃ/ Sound (as in "nation")

- **Context:** When "t" is part of a "tion" or similar suffix.
- **Examples:** nation, station, action.

The /ʃ/ sound results from the influence of "i" and "o" in certain word endings, especially those with Latin roots.

/tʃ/ Sound (as in "nature")

- **Context:** When "t" is followed by "u," forming the "ture" sound.
- **Examples:** nature, future, picture.

The combination of "t" and "u" creates a palatalized sound, merging to form /tʃ/.

Silent "T" (as in "castle")

- **Context:** Found in certain words where historical pronunciation dropped the "t" sound.
- **Examples:** castle, listen, fasten.

The silent "t" is due to the evolution of English pronunciation, where certain consonants were dropped over time.

12. The Letter "D"

"D" can change its sound or become silent in specific contexts.

/d/ Sound (as in "dog")

- **Context:** Standard pronunciation found at the start or middle of words.
- **Examples:** dog, bread, end.

The basic /d/ sound is a voiced stop, common in many words.

/dʒ/ Sound (as in "judge")

- **Context:** Occurs in words where "d" is followed by "g" or "j."
- **Examples:** judge, edge, badge.

The /dʒ/ sound happens due to the combination of "d" with certain following letters, creating a palatalized effect.

Silent "D" (as in "handsome")

- **Context:** Found in some words where the pronunciation of "d" was dropped historically.
- **Examples:** handsome, Wednesday, sandwich

Silent "d" appears in words where the letter was once pronounced but is no longer articulated.

Chapter 3: Grapheme and Phoneme Table

In this chapter, the letter sounds are treated in groups based on the ease of immediate application. This method of teaching letter sounds has been proven to be very effective by various adult literacy research work because it helps the learners to immediately understand the relationship between letters, sounds and words.

Secondly, the sounds are grouped based on certain common characteristics among the sounds' symbols (letters). For example; c, k, ck can be grouped together because they produce the same sound.

Thirdly, diagraphs (a cluster of two letters eg. ph, ea, ir, ch) or trigraphs (a cluster of three letters eg. ght, igh, are, our) are also grouped based on their related functions and sounds.

The reason for this breakdown is to ensure that the sounds are taught to the learners in chunks and in stages.

Group one

This group is made up of six sounds which are;

p, i, t, s, m, a.

The above combination makes it easy to form words using only the sounds (letters) provided in the group.

For example;
Sounds:
p, i, t, s, m, a.

Words from sounds:
pit, it, sit, Sam, I, mat, am, is, map

these words can also be used to make complete sentences.
For examples:
1. I sit
2. It is a mat
3. It is a pit
4. I am Sam
5. It is a map

This method of teaching letter sounds allows learners to immediately make meaning from what they learn.

We can agree together that this strategy is more effective compare to the traditional method of learning the letters' names and sounds and then relate the letters to objects instead of the sounds, which makes the understanding of the relationship between letters, sounds and words a bit difficult.

The same approach used to treat the sounds in "group one" is used for other groups in the table below.

Sounds	Words from Sounds	Sentences from Words
Group 1 p, i, t, s, m, a.	1. pit 2. it 3. sit 4. Sam 5. I 6. mat 7. am 8. is 9. map	a. I sit b. It is a mat c. It is a pit d. I am Sam e. It is a map
Group 2 b, e, t, n, r, d	1. bet 2. net 3. ten 4. red 5. bed 6. bend	a. Ten bets b. The bed is red c. I bet d. Bend the net

Group 3 c, o, d, g, l	1. cod 2. log 3. god 4. dog 5. cold 6. gold	a. The dog b. Cod is cold c. A gold log d. The god e. I see gold
Group 4 More activities on blending, segmentation and manipulation	Make new words from the sounds in lesson 1 & 2.	Form new sentences from words
Group 5 f, u, n, s, h	1. fun 2. sun 3. run 4. has 5. fish 6. hush	a. Fun in the sun b. I run c. She has a fish d. Hush the noise e. The sun is up

Group 6 l, a, k, e, b	1. lake 2. bake 3. leak 4. beak	a. The lake is big b. Bake a cake c. The leak d. The beak is red
Group 7 e, n, d, o, p, r, c, h, th,	1. do 2. not 3. the 4. she 5. cat 6. on 7. he 8. no	a. Do not sit b. Open the car c. She is on the mat d. He is in the car e. No cat is on the mat.
Group 8 More activities on blending, segmentation and manipulation	Make new words from the sounds in lesson 1 & 2.	Form new sentences from words

Group 9 j, i, m, n, t	1. Jim 2. tin 3. join 4. him 5. inn	a. Jim joins in b. Open the tin c. Go to the inn d. I see him e. Join me
Group 10 h, o, p, n, k	1. hop 2. no 3. on 4. pin 5. knock	a. I hop b. No pin c. Knock on d. Hop on e. I knock
Group 11 r, a, t, s, g	1. rat 2. rag 3. star 4. tar 5. tag	a. The rat b. A rag star c. Tar is black d. I see a tag e. Tag the rag

| **Group 12** More activities on blending, segmentation and manipulation | Make new words from the sounds in lesson 1, 2 & 3 | Form new sentences from the words. |

Group 13 f, u, w, j, g, y, l.	1. fan 2. up 3. will 4. jug 5. us 6. go 7. let	a. Sit up b. This is a jug c. He will sit on the mat d. Let us go e. On the fan
Group 14 w, e, l, b, x	1. web 2. bell 3. well 4. bet 5. box	a. The web b. The bell rings c. A well d. I bet e. A box
Group 15 v, o, t, m, s	1. vote 2. vet 3. most 4. Sold 5. Home	a. I vote b. The vet c. I sold it d. Home is the best e. Vote for him

Group 16 More activities on blending, segmentation and manipulation	Make new words from the sounds in lesson 1 & 2.	Form new sentences from words.

Group 17 z, e, b, u, q	1. buzz 2. zebra 3. use 4. quiz 5. cube	a. A buzz b. A zebra c. I use it d. A quiz e. A cube
Group 18 ch, a, t, c, r	1. chat 2. catch 3. rat 4. arch 5. car	a. We chat b. I catch c. A rat d. The arch e. The car
Group 19 y, a, p, l, d	1. yap 2. lad 3. play 4. day 5. pad	a. The dog yaps b. A lad plays c. It is day d. I play e. A pad

Group 20 More activities on blending, segmentation and manipulation	Make new words from the sounds in lesson 1 & 2.	Form new sentences from words
Group 21 sh, o, p, f, w **Group 22** th (voiced), e, n, k, f	1. shop 2. show 3. fish 4. wish 5. wash 1. them 2. then 4. Those	a. I shop b. A show c. A fish d. I wish e. Wash it a. I see them b. Then go c. A thin rod d. I think e. The tenth one

Group 23 th (unvoiced), a, n, k, i	1. thank 2. thin 3. think 4. path 5. bath	a. I thank b. A thin path c. I think d. The path e. A bath
Group 24 More activities on blending, segmentation and manipulation	Make new words from the sounds in lesson 1,2&3	Form new sentences from Words
Group 25 j, o, b, v, l	1. job 2. jog 3. love 4. jar 5. lobe	a. I jog b. A job c. I love d. A jar e. The lobe

Group 26	1. dog	a. The dog
d, o, g, h, n	2. god	b. Oh god
	3. nod	c. I nod
	4. hog	d. The hog
	5. don	e. Don the cap
Group 27	1. rang	a. I rang
ng, a, n, r, s	2. sang	b. I sang
	3. bang	c. A bang
	4. hang	d. Hang it
	5. gang	e. A gang
Group 28 More activities on blending, segmentation and manipulation	Make new words from the sounds in lesson 1 & 2.	Form new sentences from Words

Group 29	1. her	a. Her term
	2. term	b. In the barn
er, a, n, t, b	3. barn	c. I burn
	4. burn	d. Turn it
	5. turn	e. A term
Group 30		
zh, a, r, u, f	1. measure	a. I measure
	2. pleasure	b. It's a pleasure
	3. treasure	c. A treasure
	4. leisure	d. Leisure time
Group 31		
ow, b, r, n, s	1. bow	a. A bow
	2. row	b. A row
	3. now	c. I go now
Group 32	4. snow	d. The snow
More activities	5. town	e. The town
on blending, segmentation and manipulation	Make new words from the sounds in lesson 1 & 2.	Form new sentences from Words

Group 33 oi, b, l, n, t	1. boil 2. oil 3. loin 4. coin 5. join	a. Boil the oil b. A loin c. A coin d. Join me
Group 34 ure, f, c, s, n	1. pure 2. cure 3. sure 4. lure 5. endure	a. It's pure b. A cure c. I am sure d. A lure e. I endure
Group 35 air, f, h, b, m	1. fair 2. hair 3. bear	a. The fair b. Her hair c. A bear
Group 36 Activities on blending, segmentation and manipulation	Make new words from the sounds in lesson 1 & 2.	Form new sentences from Words

Group 37 ear, d, b, n, t	1. dear 2. hear 3. near 4. tear 5. bear	a. My dear b. I hear c. Come near d. A tear e. A bear
Group 38 ou, oa, ai, ar, oar	1. out 2. boat 3. rain 4. star 5. roar	1. Please go out and play. 2. We sailed in a boat on the lake. 3. The rain is falling heavily. 4. The star is shining brightly. 5. I heard a lion's roar in the distance.

Group 39 ea, ee, ei, ir, ie	1. eat 2. see 3. receive 4. bird 5. pie	1. I like to eat apples. 2. Can you see the rainbow? 3. Did you receive my message? 4. The bird is singing in the tree. 5. She baked a delicious pie.
Group 40 More activities on blending, segmentation and manipulation	Make new words from the sounds in lesson 1, 2 & 3	Form new sentences from Words

Group 41 oo, air, our, or, ur	1. book 2. hair 3. hour 4. fork 5. nurse	1. I read a good book last night. 2. Her hair is very long and shiny. 3. We will arrive in an hour. 4. Use a fork to eat your salad. 5. The nurse took my temperature.
Group 42 igh, tch, ph, gh, nk, eer	1. night 2. watch 3. photo 4. laugh 5. bank 6. cheer	1. The stars are visible at night. 2. I wear a watch on my wrist. 3. She took a photo of the sunset. 4. His joke made everyone laugh. 5. I need to deposit money in

		the bank. 6. The crowd began to cheer loudly.
Group 43 bl, cl, sl, pl, fl, gl	1. blue 2. clap 3. drop 4. slow 5. flag glass	1. The sky is blue 2. Clap your hands 3. Drop the key on the table 4. This car is too slow 5. The Nigerian flag has two colours 6. She needs a glass of water
Group 44 More activities on blending, segmentati	Make new words from the sounds in	Form new sentences from Words

on and manipulation	lesson 1, 2 & 3	
Group 45 th, sh, ch, wh, ph	1. this 2. shop 3. cheap 4. which 5. phone	1. This is my favourite book. 2. I went to the shop to buy groceries. 3. The shirt was cheap but of good quality. 4. Which one do you prefer? 5. I need to charge my phone.

Group 46 br, cr, dr, fr, gr, pr, wr, tr	1. broom 2. cry 3. drugs 4. fry 5. grace 6. pray 7. wrong 8. true	a. Use the long broom to sweep the floor b. Why do babies cry? c. Have you taken your drugs? d. Her name is Grace e. Pray every time f. Your answer is wrong g. What he said is true
Group 47 scr, spl, spr, str, shr, chr	1. scrap 2. shred 3. splash 4. spring 5. string	1. I need to scrap the old car. 2. Please shred these documents. 3. The kids love to splash in the pool. 4. Flowers bloom

Group 48 Thorough revision and exercises	Thorough revision and exercises	in the spring. 5. He played a melody on the guitar string. Thorough revision and exercises
Group 49 a_e e_e i_e o_e u_e **Group 50** Syllables	1. cake 2. meet 3. bite 4. go 5. cute Words and examples of syllable	1. She baked a delicious cake. 2. It's nice to meet you. 3. Be careful, the dog might bite. 4. Let's go to the park. 5. That puppy is so cute. Exercises on syllables

Group 51&52 Graphemes with similar sounds	Graphemes and use cases	Examples and exercises
Group 53&54 Punctuation	Full stop (.) Comma (,) Semicolon (;) Colon (:) Dash (-) Hyphen (-) Apostrophe (') Exclamation Mark (!) Question Mark (?) Parentheses ( ) Brackets [ ] Ellipsis (...) Slash (/)	

Chapter 4: Sound Syllables

A syllable is a part of a word that contains a single vowel with or without consonant but pronounced as a unit. The understanding of syllables is essential for accurate and fluent reading because of the following reasons;

a. It helps readers determine vowel length (long, short or diphthong).

b. It allows readers to identify patterns in endings and beginnings which can help with reading longer words.

c. It can also aid in solving spelling problems.

In order words, learning to read syllables makes decoding words more efficient.

For example, the word "cat" has one syllable, the word market has two syllables; mar - ket and the word "banana" has three syllables; ba - na - na.

Counting Syllables

1. Listen to vowels: Each syllable has one vowel sound. In some cases, consonants like "y" and "w" can function as vowels.

For example;

"y" function as a vowel in these words; "baby", "by", "cry" etc. Also "w" function as a vowel in these words; "wonderful", "how", "now", etc.

Note that the "w" sound usually creates a glide from one vowel to another.

2. Look for consonants: Often, syllables are separated by consonants. However, two consonants between vowels might split with each other going to a different syllable. E.g. hap-pen.

Syllable stress
In English, one syllable in each word is always stress more than the other. The stressed syllable is pronounced louder, longer and at a higher pitch. For example, in the word "banana" the stress is on the second syllable "ba - NA - na.

Types of Syllables

There are two types of syllables in English;
a. Open syllables: These are syllables that end with vowel sounds e.g., "he", "baby"
b. Closed syllables: These are syllables that end with consonants e.g., "cat", "sit".

Syllables Rules

a. Dividing words: When dividing words into syllables, every syllable must have at least one vowel.
b. Consonant + "le": When a word ends in "le" preceded by a consonant, the "le" is a separate syllable e.g. "lit-tle".
c. Double consonant: The double consonants in some words often split between syllables e.g. "but - ter".

Chapter 5: Levels of Phonemic Awareness

The Six Levels of Phonemic Awareness

These six abilities serve as the building blocks for phonemic awareness and are essential for the development of effective listening comprehension skills. Without a solid grasp of these abilities, readers can struggle with decoding, spelling, and reading fluency.

1. Phoneme Isolation

The ability to isolate and identify the individual sounds (phonemes) that make up a word, such as the initial /b/ sound in bag or the final /k/ sound in look.

For example:

a. The first sound in cat is /c/, the second sound is /a/, and the last sound is /t/.

b. The first sound in fish is /f/, the second sound is /i/, and the last sound is /sh/.

c. The first sound in eat is /ea/, and the last sound is /t/.

2. Phoneme Blending
The ability to merge separate phonemes together to form a word, like combining the individual sounds /c/ /a/ /t/ into the word cat.

For example:
a. /m/ /a/ /t/ - mat
b. /r/ /oa/ /d/ - road
c. /k/ /i/ /ck/ - kick

3. Phoneme Segmentation
The ability to pull the sounds out of a word. It is the ability to break words down into their component phonemes, for instance, breaking "cat" into /c/, /a/, and /t/.

For Example:
a. The word "law" contains two sounds, /l/ and /aw/

b. The word "car" contains two sounds, /c/ and /ar/

c. The word "phone" contains three sounds, /ph/, /o/ and /ne/

4. Phoneme Addition

The ability to add phonemes to a word to create a new word, like adding /m/ to "tea" to get "team."
For Example:
a. add /r/ to "pea" to get "pear."
b. add /h/ to "old" to get "hold."
a. add /c/ to "fat" to get "fact."

5. Phoneme Deletion

The ability to remove a phoneme from a word, resulting in a new word. For example, deleting the /k/ sound from "book" to create "boo."
For Example:

a. delete /m/ from "farm" to get "far"

b. delete /w/ from "now" to get "no"

c. delete /r/ from "driver" to get "drive"

6. Phoneme Substitution

The ability to replace a phoneme within a word, generating a new word in the process. For example, switching the /p/ sound for an /s/ sound in "pot" to create "sot."

For Example:

a. Change /f/ in "few" to /d/ it becomes "dew"

b. Change /u/ in "cup" to /a/ it becomes "cap"

c. Change /d/ in "load" to /f/ it becomes "loaf"

Graphemes with Similar Sounds

A grapheme is a visual symbol or letter that represents a specific sound or group of sounds in a language. For example, in the English language, the letter "a" is a grapheme that can represent the sound /æ/ in words like "cat" or the sound /eɪ/ in words like "cake."

/b/	/k/	/ch/	/f/	/j/	/m/	/n/	/ng/	/r/	/s/
lb	c	tch	ph	g	lm	kn	n(k)	wr	c
bb	ch			dge	mn	ng			sc
	ck				mb				
	x				__me				
	qu								

/sh/	/v/	/w/	/e/	/i/	/o/	/u/	/ai/	/ei/
Ch	ve	wh	ea	ee	oa	o	igh	a
t(ion)			ai	ey	o / _e		ie	ai
s(ion, ure)			ay	y	ow		i_e	
ss(ion,ure)				e			i	
c(ion, ious, ial)				ea			ei	
				e_e				
				ie				
				eo				

/air/	/ear/	/oi/	/ar/	/or/	/ur/	/oar/	/our/	/ure/
Are	eer	oy	a	aw	er	u	a	u
Ear	ere		are	au	ir			
Ere				ore	ear			
				oor				
				our				

Chapter 6: Introduction to Sight Words

Examples of Sight Words

Sight words are frequently used words in verbal and communication.

Level 1:

A	and	away	big
Blue	can	come	down
Find	for	funny	go
Help	here	I	in
Is	it	jump	little
Look	make	me	my
Not	one	play	red
Run	said	see	the

| Three | to | two | up |
| we | where | yellow | you |

Level 2:

All	am	are	at
Ate	be	black	brown
But	came	did	do
Eat	four	get	good
Have	he	into	like
Must	new	no	now
on	our	out	please
pretty	ran	ride	saw
say	she	so	soon
that	there	they	this
too	under	want	was
well	went	what	white

| who | will | with | yes |

Level 3:

after	again	an	any
as	ask	by	could
every	fly	from	give
going	had	has	her
him	his	how	just
know	let	live	may
of	old	once	open
over	put	round	some
stop	take	thank	them
then	think	walk	were

Sight Words Sentences

I see a cat.	The dog is big.
It is hot.	Come here.
It is fun.	It's time for bed.
What's your name?	Where is the car?
The train is loud.	He likes to read.
She is my friend.	The sun is shining.
I like to play with my toys.	

The cat is soft.

Can you see the bird in the sky?

The bunny hops.

I want a blue crayon.

The baby is sleeping.

We eat yummy food.

I can draw a circle.

It's time for lunch.

The dog barks loudly.

The book has pictures.

The car is fast.

The moon is out at night.

I have a new bike.

The frog is on a lily pad.

Sentence Formation

A sentence is a group of words that are put together to make a complete thought.

All sentences include two parts:

a. Subject: the person or thing that the sentence is about. It's like the topic of the sentence.

b. Predicate: this contains what is said about the subject.

Note: the predicate must contain a verb.

Example of sentences

Subject	Predicate	
	Verb	

The man	is	A police officer
She	sells	Foodstuff in the market
My car	has	Flat tyre

Note also that a sentence begins with a capital letter and ends with a full stop or a question mark or an exclamation mark. Look at these examples:

People need food.
How are you?
Look out!

Chapter 7: **Punctuation**

Punctuation refers to the marks or symbols used in writing to clarify the meaning and structure of text. It helps readers understand the relationships between words, phrases, and clauses, and it also assists in conveying tone, emphasis, and rhythm. Here is a breakdown of the main punctuation marks and their uses:

1. Full Stop (.)
Also known as a period, it marks the end of a sentence.
Example: I like reading books.

2. Comma (,)
Separates items in a list, sets off nonessential clauses, and indicates a pause in the flow of a sentence.
Example: I like reading books, watching movies, and playing games.

3. Semicolon (;)
Separates two independent clauses that are closely related in meaning.
Example: I have visited many cities in my lifetime; Paris is my favourite.

4. Colon (:)
Introduces a list, a quotation, or an explanation.

Example: I have three favourite foods: pizza, sushi, and tacos.

5. Dash (-)

Indicates a break in thought or sets off a parenthetical remark.

Example: I was planning to go to the store - but then I forgot my wallet.

6. Hyphen (-)

Joins two or more words together to form a compound word or indicates a range.

Example: self-made, Monday-Friday.

7. Exclamation Mark (!)

Indicates strong emotions or emphasis.

Example: I love reading books!

8. Question Mark (?)
Indicates a question.
Example: Do you like reading books?

9. Apostrophe (')
Indicates possession or forms contractions.
Example: The cat's toy, don't.

10. Quotation Marks ("")
Sets off direct quotations or dialogue.
Example: "I love reading books," said the student.

11. Parentheses ( )
Sets off information that's not essential to the meaning of a sentence.

Example: I like reading books (especially fiction).

12. Brackets [ ]
Used to add information to a quotation or clarify meaning.
Example: "I love reading books [especially fiction]."

13. Ellipsis (...)
Indicates a pause or omission of words in a quotation.
Example: "I love reading books... especially fiction."

14. Slash (/)
Indicates a choice between two words or phrases.
Example: Akwa Ibomites don't eat dogs. True/False

Chapter 5: Reading Comprehension

Lesson 5.1. Vocabulary Building

Vocabulary building involves expanding your word knowledge to improve comprehension and communication. A robust vocabulary allows you to understand texts more deeply and express yourself more clearly.

When to focus on Vocabulary Building:

1. When encountering unfamiliar words frequently.
2. When wanting to improve overall language skills.

3. When preparing for standardized tests or professional exams.

How to Build Vocabulary:
1. Read Regularly. Exposure to diverse materials introduces you to new words.
2. Use a Dictionary. Look up unfamiliar words and understand their meanings.
3. Keep a Vocabulary Journal. Write down new words, their definitions, and example sentences.
4. Practice Usage. Use new words in your writing and speaking to reinforce your memory.
5. Learn Word Roots, Prefixes, and Suffixes. Understanding the components of words can help

you deduce the meanings of new words.

Example:
While reading a novel, you come across the word "ambiguous." You look it up, find it means "open to more than one interpretation," write it in your vocabulary journal, and try to use it in a sentence like "The ending of the movie was ambiguous, leaving viewers to form their own conclusions."

Developing Fluency

Passage Reading Challenge
Read and re-read the passage. Re-reading passages is the main way to learn fluency.

Reading Passages

Day one

Title: Shopping for Clothes

I like shopping for new clothes. I went to the store and found a stylish dress. It fits me perfectly. Fashion lets me express my personality.

Day two

Title: My Place of Worship
I go to a place of worship every week. It's important to me. I pray and find peace there. Religion helps me connect with something greater than myself.

Day three

Title: A Family Gathering
Every Sunday, my family gathers for dinner. We share stories and laugh together. Spending time with family is important to me. It makes me feel loved and connected.

Day four

Title: Choosing Outfits
In the morning, I choose my outfit. I like to wear clothes that make me feel good. Fashion is a way to express myself. Today, I picked a blue shirt and comfortable jeans.

Day five
Title: Staying Active
I go for a walk every morning. Walking keeps me healthy and strong. Exercise is good for my body and mind. It's important to take care of our health.

Day six

Title: Being a Good Friend
Being a good friend is important to me. I listen when my friends talk. I help them when they need it. Building strong relationships make life better.

Day seven

Title: Eating Mindfully
I practice eating mindfully. I take my time to savor each bite. It helps me enjoy my meals and makes me more aware of the food I eat. Mindful eating is a healthy habit.

Day eight

Title: Starting a Healthy Routine

I decided to start a healthy routine. I wake up early to exercise. I eat fresh fruits and vegetables. It's important to take care of my health. I feel better every day.

Day nine

Title: The Itam Market

Every weekend, I visit the Itam market. People sell all sorts of things there. I enjoy finding treasures and meeting friendly

sellers. Buying and selling can be fun and exciting.
Day ten

Title: Maria's Flower Shop
Maria has a small flower shop. She sells colourful flowers to people in the neighbourhood. Her flowers make people smile. Maria works hard to make her small business successful. She loves helping others with her beautiful flowers.

Activities

Activity 1
Greet and introduce yourself in the following situations:
1. Meeting with someone for the first time.
2. Introduce yourself before a large audience.
3. Advertise your skills or profession.

Activity 2
1. Write the alphabet letters from A-Z. Both the uppercase and the lowercase.

2. Circle only the vowels letters.

Activity 3
Circle the graphemes that have the same phoneme as the one provided below.

1. / k /	-	m	⒞	p	ⒸⓀ	ⒸⒽ	
2. / j /	-	d	dge	f	g	s	
3. / m /	-	l	l	mn	_mb	u	
4. / i /	-	m	ee	or	ea	y	
5. / or /	-	u	air	aw	eo	au	
		o					
		o					
		r					

Activity 4
Group these graphemes based on their phonemes similarity:
oa, i, o, igh, c, o_e, k, ck,

| oa, o, o_e | i, igh | c, k, ck |

1. f, b, c, _lb, sc, eer, ph, s, ear

| | | |

2. our, ai, oar, i, ei, or, a, ey, u,

| | | |

3. ch, ir, are, tch, wr, sh, r, ar, ur

| | | |

Activity 5
Circle the phonemes that do not belong to the group:

1. ir   er   (wr)   ear

1. ar   yoo   ui   ew
2. ee   ay   e   i
3. aw   or   er   o
4. ss   sc   ce   qu

5. t   j   g   dge

6. qu   k   z   c
7. n   kn   m   gn
8. Ph   ks   f   gh
9. a   ei   ai   oi

Activity 6

Write out the first and the last sound of the following words:

1. Cheap   -   <u>ch</u>   <u>p</u>
2. Eating -   _____   _____
3. Sent   -   _____   _____
4. Pack   -   _____   _____
5. Phone   -   _____   _____
6. Wish   -   _____   _____
7. Write   -   _____   _____
8. High   -   _____   _____
9. Calm   -   _____   _____
10. Comb   -   _____   _____